P9-AGI-311

JEWELED BUGS
Jeweled Bugs

AND *and* BUTTERFLIES

Marilyn Nissenson and Susan Jonas

Harry N. Abrams, Inc., Publishers

Editor: Harriet Whelchel
Designer: Carol Robson

Library of Congress Cataloging-in-Publication Data

Nissenson, Marilyn, 1939–
  Jeweled bugs and butterflies / Marilyn Nissenson and Susan Jonas.
    p. cm.
  Includes index.
  ISBN 0–8109–3523–6
  1. Jewelry. 2. Butterflies in art. 3. Insects in art. I. Jonas, Susan.
II. Title.
  NK7306.N57 2000
  739.27'8–dc21
                                            99-36663

Text copyright © 2000 Marilyn Nissenson and Susan Jonas
Illustrations copyright © 2000 Harry N. Abrams, Inc.

Published in 2000 by Harry N. Abrams, Incorporated, New York
All rights reserved. No part of the contents of this book may be
reproduced without the written permission of the publisher

Printed and bound in Hong Kong

Harry N. Abrams, Inc.
100 Fifth Avenue
New York, N.Y. 10011
www.abramsbooks.com

Binding front: Hatpin. René Lalique, French, 1897–99. Enamel and gold, 7" high. Collection David Weinstein. Photograph by Sotheby's, London

Endpapers: See pages 28–29, 97 below, 107 top

Page 1: Spider brooch. American, c. 1900. Gold, platinum, diamonds, rubies, and demantoid garnets, 1¼" diameter. Private Collection

Pages 2–3: Insect stickpins. Primarily American, c. 1900. Gold, enamels, and stones, 3 x 1½–1¾". Private Collection

Opposite: Butterfly brooch. Gabriella Kiss, American, 1990s. Bronze and 22-karat gold, 1 x 5". J. Mavec & Co., New York

CONTENTS

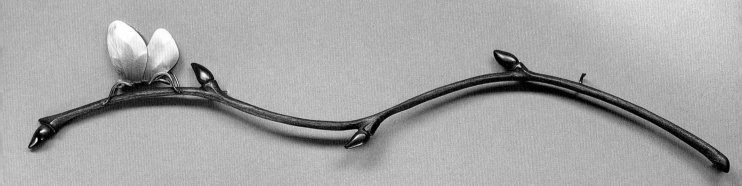

INTRODUCTION

*We marvel at elephants' shoulders carrying castles, and bulls' necks
and the fierce tossings of their heads, at the rapacity of tigers and the
manes of lions, whereas really Nature is to be found in her entirety
nowhere more than in her smallest creatures.*
—Pliny the Elder, *Natural History* II: 435

Membership in the Order of the Golden Fly was a coveted honor in Middle
Kingdom Egypt. Pharaohs gave gold pendants in the shape of a fly to their most
valiant soldiers and assiduous civil servants. Plagued as they were by swarms
of flies, the ancient Egyptians had studied the insects closely and grudgingly
admired them for their swift maneuverability and their persistence. The
Egyptians also made gods of scorpions and mosquitoes—either to placate
these pests or to take on their attributes—and of the dung beetle for its association with death and rebirth.

Fly pendants from the tomb of Queen Aahhotep.
Egyptian, early 18th Dynasty (c. 1540 B.C.). Gold,
each fly 2 ⅝" high. Egyptian Museum, Cairo

The pendants were part of an award for valor,
perhaps reflecting the role Queen Aahhotep played
in the war of independence against the Hyksos
rulers of Egypt.

Like virtually every culture that followed, Egyptians recognized that few
animals have a closer relationship with humans than insects do. For one thing,
they are all around us. More than half of all the known species of animals,

plants, and microorganisms on Earth are insects. At least 750,000 species of insects have been identified, and there are probably millions more lurking unnoticed in jungles and forests.

In the 1930s, Frank Lutz, a curator at the American Museum of Natural History in New York, surveying a 75-by-200-foot garden plot in suburban New Jersey, counted 1,402 insect species. He found 467 different species of butterflies and moths, 258 species of flies, 259 of beetles, and 167 of wasps, bees, and ants. Dr. Kefyn M. Catley, a scientist at the museum today, speculates that in a conventional backyard, where the single crop of grass would be more limiting to species diversity than a garden, there might be 25 to 50 large, easily visible arthropod species represented on the surface or in the grass. However, says Dr. Catley, only a few inches below the surface, are tens of thousands of individual creatures—most of them barely visible to the naked eye.

Scientists like Lutz and Catley are careful to distinguish between members of the class Insecta and their cousins in the class Arachnida. All are members of the phylum Arthropoda, but insects have three body parts—head, thorax, and abdomen—and six jointed legs, whereas arachnids, among them the spiders, scorpions, mites, and ticks, have eight legs and only two body parts—the cephalothorax and the abdomen. Adding to the confusion is the fact that although all bugs are insects, not all insects are bugs. Only members of the suborder Hemiptera—stinkbugs, bedbugs, squash bugs, among others—are true bugs. As the name of their suborder would imply, the hind set of wings of true bugs are so thin they look like half wings. In practice, most people call the whole lot of creeping, crawling, flying, buzzing small creatures *bugs* or *insects* interchangeably.

Insects probably first appeared on Earth sometime in the middle of the Paleozoic era, some 350 to 400 million years ago, but they became abundant only with the emergence of flowering plants, during the Cretaceous period around 120 million years ago.

Insects are the only class of animals that has adapted to all climates and environments. They can live at altitudes higher than 15,000 feet, on frozen tundra, in fresh and brackish water, in caves where there is no light. They can live in petroleum and formaldehyde, and in hot springs, where the temperature approaches the boiling point. Although relatively few insects live in oceans, one hardy species lives in the nostrils of sea lions.

Insects range in size from minute fungus beetles, which are smaller than the head of a pin, to the foot-long walking stick from the Malay Peninsula. Another giant, the Hercules moth of Australia, has a wingspan of more than fourteen inches.

Insects are the natural competitors of humankind. They feed on our crops, on domesticated animals, and on timber; they make their homes in our houses and share our breakfast cereals. Some insects depend on our blood as their source of nourishment.

We are more likely to overlook the fact that they are also our chief allies. Without insects there would be no silk, no honey, no potatoes; insects pollinate fruit trees, flowers, cotton plants, and hundreds of other crops. They clean up the earth's surface by feeding on decaying material. Their cousins, the spiders, are the world's most dominant carnivores in terms of both the biomass and the total number of species they feed on that would otherwise attack crops and spread disease. Without the entire complement of insects and arachnids, the world as we know it would be unrecognizable within months.

Because human beings have lived intimately and interdependently with insects, and have observed their behavior and their life cycles so closely, many cultures have incorporated attributes of insects in their myths and folklore. People make powerful symbols or metaphors of them. Spiders pull strings behind the scene; ants soldier on diligently; moths are drawn to the flame.

The metamorphosis of a butterfly or a cicada from the immature to the adult state has symbolized birth, death, resurrection, and rebirth for peoples as various as the ancient Egyptians and Native Americans. In general, butterflies are a sign of good luck; however, to some people, their ability to change shape seems more ominous, more like the power of a witch or the devil, and they are, therefore, an omen of death. Bronze Age Greeks, Chinese, and pre-Hispanic

Insect necklet. Elsa Schiaparelli, French, 1938. Plastic and metal, 8¼ x 7½". Brooklyn Museum of Art, Gift of Paul and Arturo Peralta-Ramos, Brooklyn, New York

8

cultures believed that butterflies, flying free after their previous earthbound existence, symbolize the soul.

The impulse to observe closely insects in nature has persisted from ancient times to the present, but during the Renaissance, people began to look at nature not only for its religious or symbolic applications, but also for its own sake. In the early sixteenth century, western Europe was swept by a passion for collecting natural objects. Wealthy merchants and scholars competed to fill their *wunderkammen,* or "cabinets of curiosities," with artifacts, familiar and strange, amassed from around the world. Collected specimens of natural history, ranging from bits of coral to volcanic rocks to rare moths, were mounted side by side with ancient coins and contemporary paintings. The impulse of these early collectors was to be encyclopedic; it was based on the belief that man was at the center of the universe and had the capacity to know and understand everything.

The increasingly sophisticated obsession with the classification of plant and animal species—fed in the eighteenth century by the Enlightenment and based on the taxonomic system devised by Carolus Linnaeus—continued unabated into the nineteenth century. No middle-class parlor was complete without a glass-covered box of mounted entomological specimens: insects were a popular favorite, whether gorgeous butterflies or equally gorgeous but more unsettling beetles, earwigs, or praying mantises.

Easily the best-known insect collector in the twentieth century was Vladimir Nabokov, an ardent butterfly expert who tracked down rare species and named them with the same combination of whimsy and esoteric knowledge that characterized much of his fiction. Less renowned for his fieldwork but no less devoted to insects was Salvador Dalí, who often carried live beetles with him to social engagements. Dalí made insects a recurrent motif in many paintings: grasshoppers in *Myself at the Age of Ten When I Was the Grasshopper Child,* daddy longlegs in *Daddy Longlegs of the Evening—Hope!* as well as ants in *Accommodations of Desire, Portrait of Gala,* and *Great Masturbator.*

Until the nineteenth century, the use of insects in jewelry was largely symbolic. Noble families occasionally took insects like grasshoppers, beetles, and butterflies as their totem. The patrician Barberini family of seventeenth-century Rome and the Bonaparte dynasty in the nineteenth century adopted the bee as their symbol, perhaps to indicate family virtues of determination and hard work.

The eighteenth-century fascination with natural images in jewelry design, which first manifested itself in jeweled flowers, led jewelers at the turn of the century to incorporate decorative insect designs—most commonly of butterflies—on lockets, necklaces, and brooches. The next step was a veritable plague of bejeweled wasps, earwigs, flies, stag beetles, and spiders, which began to crawl over bodices, hats, and veils in the 1860s. Perhaps the designers of this jewelry were motivated by a love of the macabre, perhaps by the notion that there is beauty to be found in every living thing, or perhaps they took a salacious pleasure in adorning a woman with a creature that she would likely be loath to touch in nature.

Although dried scarabs were sometimes incorporated into jewelry, actual insects were avoided. In *The Art of Beauty and the Art of Dress* (1878), Eliza Hawes wrote:

> It ought to be considered what sort of things are suited for personal adornment, and how they ought to be treated. The thing should be beautiful in itself, and it should be beautiful for you. . . . For instance, a large dried butterfly, though beautiful in itself, would not be beautiful for you—as a headdress: its wings clasping the head, its antennae surmounting it. The result will convey a painful sense of instability, fragility, and incongruousness. Whilst leaning against a cushion, the wings would crush and shatter; the very stillness of the wood creature on a human head, and in a vitiated atmosphere, would outrage the possibility of nature; thus a butterfly should always be treated conventionally and in an absolutely different material, such as metal.

After Commodore Matthew Perry paved the way for the opening of trade between the West and Japan in the 1850s, a mania for things Japanese swept Europe. Western artists were exposed for the first time to Japanese prints, textiles, and ceramics. They were awed by the simplicity of design, the economy of line, and the use of asymmetry that characterize the work of the Japanese masters. They were especially responsive to the Japanese emphasis on the natural world and the way it was often expressed in one exquisitely detailed bird, tree, flower, or insect. The Japanese aesthetic, expressed in materials previously unfamiliar to Western artists, had a powerful impact on all the decorative arts, including jewelry. Jewelry designers continued to be as fascinated with images from nature as their predecessors had been, but Japanese art suggested a way to escape from Victorian imitative realism and its insistence on formal, symmetrical ornaments set with precious gems. The resulting revolution in jewelry design made one of the most exciting contributions to what came to be known as the Art Nouveau movement.

Art Nouveau took its name from a shop called La Maison de L'Art Nouveau, which was opened in Paris in 1895 by Samuel Bing, who had been a dealer in Asian objects. Among the artists who contributed to Bing's opening exhibition was René Lalique (1860–1945). Although the movement included such talented jewelry designers as Lucien Gaillard, Eugène Feuillâtre, and Henri Vever, none surpassed Lalique in the quality and audacity of his work.

As a child, Lalique had spent hours sketching plants and insects in his native Champagne; he was familiar with insects of the meadow, such as butterflies, wasps, bumblebees, and beetles, and with the dragonflies that hovered near local ponds. Like the Japanese, he was interested in the life cycle of plants and animals, and therefore in the transience of living things. Lalique's jewelry seems remarkably atmospheric, evoking the passing seasons, times of day, even moods and emotions: two grasshoppers rest on a plum tree branch suffused by a warm golden light (pages 24-25); a swarm of wasps feeds on an opal flower head raked by a blood-orange sunset (page 71); a blue glass bee alights upon an abalone flower glistening as if it had been bathed by a late afternoon shower (page 65).

Like many of his peers, Lalique was particularly interested in the versatility of enamels, which he employed with varying degrees of opacity, translucence, transparency, and opalescence. Art Nouveau enameling techniques mirrored the actual structure of insect wings: wings are strengthened and hold their form because of a network of tiny tubes, called veins. In jeweled insects, veining is supplied by metal cell walls. In *champlevé* enameling, the cell walls are created when a metal surface is hollowed out, leaving depressions into which enamels are laid and then fired. In *cloisonné* work, wire cell walls, or *cloisons,* are soldered to a metal base and filled with enamels. In either of these two techniques, the fired enamels—however vividly colored—are opaque. *Plique-à-jour* enamels are translucent. *Plique-à-jour* enameling is a variant of *cloisonné* in which the metal base is removed after firing, and the enamel remains in suspension between the *cloisons. Plique-à-jour* enamels most closely mimic the gossamer quality and subtle gradations of color in an actual insect wing.

Art Nouveau jewelry was extraordinarily popular. The influence of the movement soon spread beyond Paris, notably to Brussels, where Philippe Wolfers (1858–1929) created astonishing dragonflies, butterflies, and flowers. Wolfers's delicacy of colors and deft use of raw materials made him almost as famous in his time as Lalique. In New York, Louis Comfort Tiffany (1848–1933) experimented at his studio with most daring Art Nouveau design at the same time that his family's store was still specializing in more traditional pieces.

Art Nouveau jewelry was produced in relatively large quantities; pieces by renowned artists inspired the manufacture of what was essentially costume jewelry. Some of these copies were distinguished in their own right. The combination of fine design and inexpensive materials reached an apogee with the French firm of Piel Frères. Although Piel Frères utilized high-quality enamel, its designers substituted celluloid for ivory, and copper and silver gilt for gold, to keep the price within range of many middle-class consumers.

In a way, Art Nouveau was a victim of its own success. The spread of cheap imitations made what had seemed revolutionary overexposed within a decade. Even at its best, much of the jewelry was quite massive and so flamboyant that only the most theatrical of women were comfortable wearing it. The inevitable reaction against Art Nouveau was also fueled by changing times: the Belle

Epoque was effaced by the age of the airplane and the automobile and the spirit of modernism. Very soon Art Deco designers jettisoned natural images in favor of geometric, streamlined forms. Yet bugs and butterflies were always too fascinating to be ignored completely. During the 1920s, Cartier, for example, created remarkable jeweled insects. The firm's winged scarab brooches were probably influenced by the opening of Tutankhamen's tomb in 1922.

In the decades after World War II, Cartier, Mauboussin, Boivin, and other fine jewelers produced a number of butterflies and dragonflies in gold, platinum, and gemstones. They also had success with earrings and brooches in the form of enameled ladybugs. The ladybug seems to be, uniquely, a beetle with a positive image. Ladybugs and their offspring prey on destructive insects; their round, compact shape is nonthreatening; and their polka-dot pattern is cheerful. They are cute, a claim few insects can make.

Contemporary jewelers continue to produce bugs and butterflies. John Paul Miller, who revived the ancient technique of granulation, in which tiny gold balls are painstakingly fused onto a surface, has been creating insect jewelry since the 1950s. His gold and enamel moths, spiders, beetles, and fly larvae are so detailed that they appear to be faithful reproductions of living species, even though they are, in fact, only suggested by nature.

Daniel Brush is an artist who also works in granulated gold. Brush makes his own alloys of gold, creates naturally magnetized steel, and handcrafts all his tools. His gold and steel dragonflies hover so delicately at the rim of steel boxes and bowls that one feels they could fly off any second.

Every year, thousands of insect species are newly identified and classified. Every year, jewelers create beautiful variations on nature's themes. Elegant, daring, sinister, even amusing—jeweled bugs and butterflies remind us that we are surrounded by natural creatures. They allow us to admire nature's ingenuity and yet keep the threatening aspects of the real world at bay.

Bee and butterfly brooch. English, 1870–80. Gold, diamonds, rubies, and enamel, 1¼ x 2¼". Private Collection

Creepy Crawlers

We know they're out there, even if we can't see them. They lurk in the grass, hop out at inopportune times, and make noise in the woods at night. We don't normally think of them as flying, and many are essentially terrestrial, but if they fly in huge swarms, they can be terrifying and devastating. They range from the true bugs like ladybugs (order Hemiptera), to beetles (Coleoptera), cicadas (Homoptera), praying mantises and grasshoppers (Orthoptera), as well as spiders and scorpions, which are arachnids.

Beetles make up the largest single order in the animal kingdom, with as many as a million different species. There are more species of beetles than of all plant species combined. In fact, about one of every four animal species known on Earth is a beetle. When asked what his studies of nature had revealed about the mind of God, J. B. S. Haldane, the noted British biologist, is reported to have said that the Lord must have "an inordinate fondness for beetles."

Spiders are generally associated with luck. In England it is considered bad luck to brush a spider from your clothing, and very bad luck to kill one. The Chippewa hung a dream catcher—a netted hoop resembling a spiderweb—to a baby's cradleboard to trap any bad dreams that might fall from the sky. For some Southwest American Indians, the spider is the Creator, who wove the web of the universe.

Scorpions are equally powerful in legend, but usually in a malevolent way. In classical legends, Scorpion is the monster that stung Orion to death and terrified the horses of the Sun, causing the crash that killed Phaeton. Many ancient cultures placed the constellation Scorpio in their zodiac, and in general it is a troubling sign, frequently associated with darkness and confusion.

On the whole, creepy crawlers are perceived as among the most disagreeable of creatures. Therefore, it is especially arresting to see them in bejeweled splendor.

Preceding pages:
Ladybug brooch and earring set. Tiffany, American, 1935. Carved crystal, gold, enamel, and diamonds, *brooch:* 1½ x 2¼", *earrings:* 1 x 1". James Robinson, Inc., New York

Opposite:
Tarantula brooch. Crane & Theurer, American, c. 1905. Gold, diamonds, and enamel, 2½" long. Private Collection

Spider brooch. American, 1950s. Mabe pearl, gold, rubies, and sapphires, 2" long. Primavera Gallery, New York

Opposite: Spider pin. American, c. 1900. Gold, moonstone, and rubies, 1⅛ x ¾". Private Collection

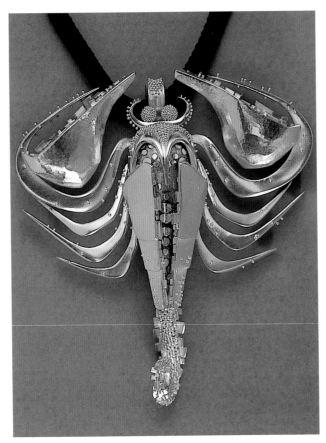

Left: Imperial beetle pendant/brooch. John Paul Miller, American, 1980s. Eighteen-karat yellow gold with enamel on pure gold, 2¼" high. Private Collection

Above: Scorpion pendant/brooch. John Paul Miller, American, 1970. Eighteen-karat yellow gold with enamel on pure gold, 3" high. Private Collection

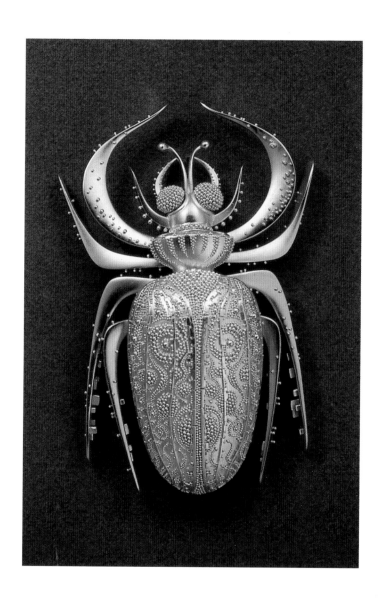

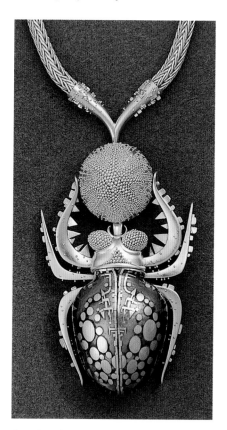

Left: Beetle pendant/brooch. John Paul Miller, American, 1995. Eighteen-karat yellow gold with enamel on pure gold, 3" high. Private Collection

Above: Dung beetle pendant/brooch. John Paul Miller, American, 1989. Eighteen-karat gold with enamel on pure gold, 3" high. Private Collection

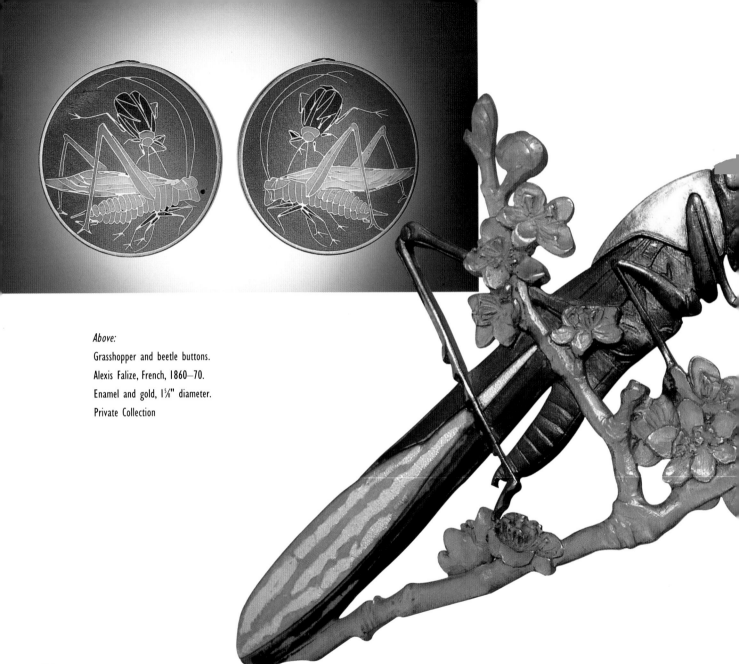

Above:
Grasshopper and beetle buttons.
Alexis Falize, French, 1860—70.
Enamel and gold, 1⅝" diameter.
Private Collection

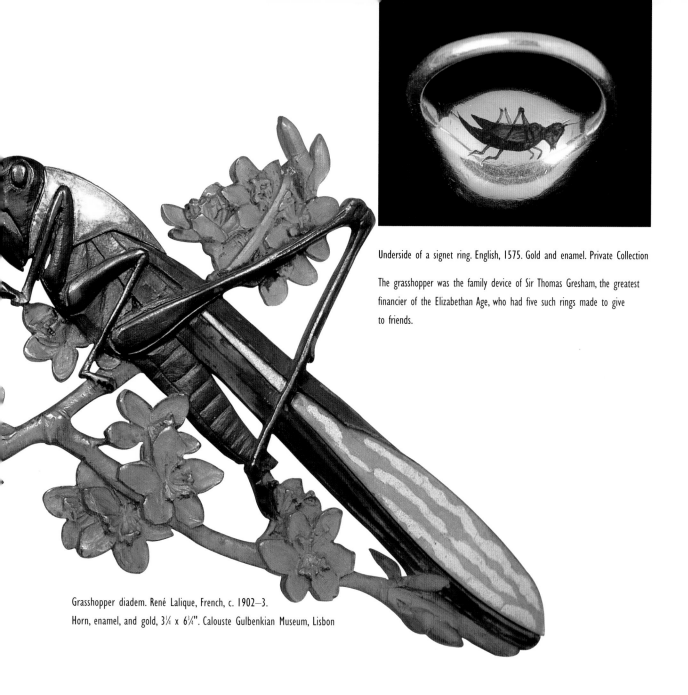

Underside of a signet ring. English, 1575. Gold and enamel. Private Collection

The grasshopper was the family device of Sir Thomas Gresham, the greatest financier of the Elizabethan Age, who had five such rings made to give to friends.

Grasshopper diadem. René Lalique, French, c. 1902–3.
Horn, enamel, and gold, 3¼ x 6¼". Calouste Gulbenkian Museum, Lisbon

Beetle brooch. English, c. 1880. Tigereye, diamonds, and gold, 2½" long.
J. Mavec & Co., New York

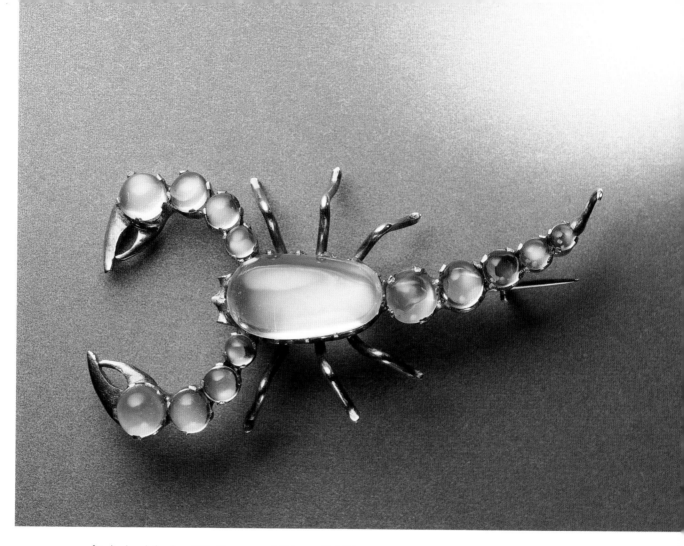

Scorpion brooch. American, 1930s. Moonstones and 14-karat gold, 1¾" long. James Robinson, Inc., New York

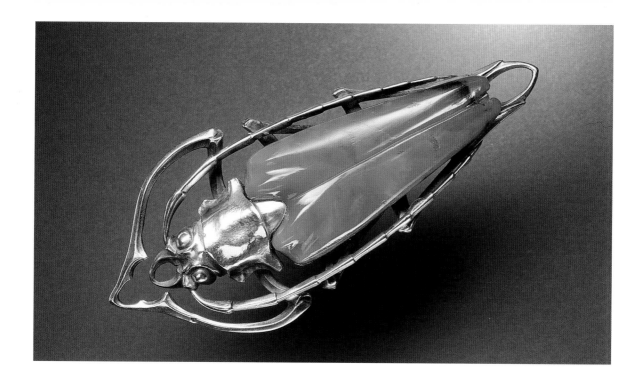

Opposite:
Beetle clips.
Hermès, French,
1960s. Coral,
onyx, and gold,
2½ x 1".
Primavera Gallery,
New York

Above:
Beetle brooch.
Lucien Gaillard,
French, c. 1900.
Amazonite and
silver, 3½ x 1½".
Macklowe Gallery
& Modernism,
New York

Right:
Ladybug earrings.
Cartier, French,
1936. Platinum,
white gold, coral,
black lacquer,
and diamonds,
¾ x ⅝". Art of
Cartier Collection,
Geneva

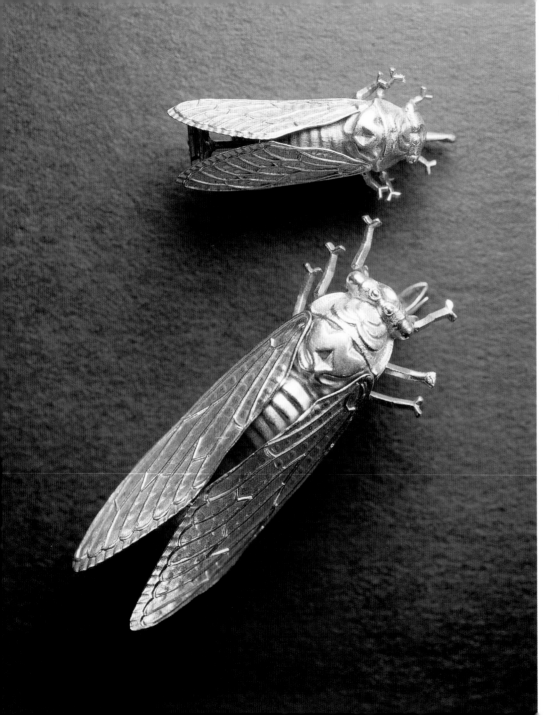

Left:
Cicada pins. Henri Guerard,
French, c. 1885.
Gold, 1¼ x ½", ¾ x ¼".
Primavera Gallery, New York

Opposite:
Cicada brooch. Boucheron,
French, c. 1880—90. Gold,
silver, diamonds, sapphires,
cabochon chrysoberyl
cat's-eyes, *champlevé* and
plique-à-jour enamel,
1⅛ x 4". Private Collection

The wings are mounted
en tremblant, so that
with any movement of the
brooch they vibrate,
simulating the buzzing of
the cicada.

Right: Beetle brooch. Verdura, American, 1990s.
Gold and pink lapis, 1½ x 1". Verdura, New York

Right: Beetle watch. Swiss, mid-19th century.
Gold, enamel, and jewels, 2⅛" long.
The Metropolitan Museum of Art.
Bequest of Laura Frances Hearn, 1917 (17.101.55)

The wings, which are movable, fold back to form
the cover of the watch.

Praying mantis brooch. American,
c. 1940. Paste on chrome, 3 x 4½".
Kentshire Galleries, New York

Praying mantis pin. Gabriella Kiss, American,
1990s. Eighteen-karat gold, 4½" long.
J. Mavec & Co., New York

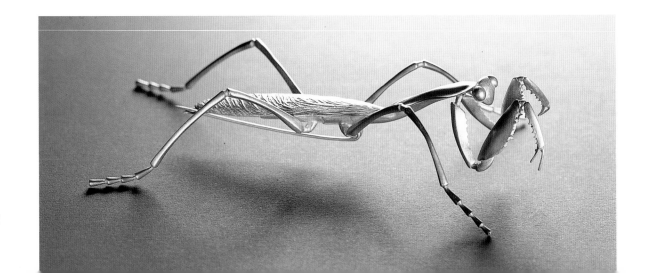

Tarantula brooch. Andreas von Zadora-Gerlof, Canadian, 1998. Gold, diamonds, emeralds, and enamel, 4⅛ x 3½". A La Vieille Russie, New York

Opposite:

Earplug in form of spider with web. Moche (Loma Negra, Peru), 1st–3rd century A.D. Gold, 3⅜" diameter. The Metropolitan Museum of Art, The Michael C. Rockefeller Memorial Collection, Bequest of Nelson A. Rockefeller, 1979 (1979.206.1240)

The Moche people were master metalsmiths; the spiderweb was cut from a single sheet of gold. The original inlays for the spider's eyes and indentations in its body are now missing.

Insect brooch. American, 1940s. Copper, 3½ x 2". Private Collection

Above:

Spider purse. LaCloche, French, c. 1920. Eighteen-karat white gold, diamond, and pearl on gold mesh, with 18-karat yellow gold chain, 3 x 3". Private Collection

Left:
Beetle and fern comb.
René Lalique, French,
c. 1902–3. Carved
horn, gold, and seed
pearls, 7 x 4".
Courtesy Sotheby's,
London

Below:
Beetle brooch.
Designed by Georg Kleemann
for Theodor Fahrner, 1902.
Gold, turquoise, emeralds,
rubies, pearl shells,
pearl, and enamel,
1⅛ x 1⅞"
Schmuckmuseum,
Pforzheim, Germany

Above: Blister beetle corsage ornament.
René Lalique, French, c. 1903–4.
Gold, glass, enamel, silver, and tourmaline,
1⅛ x 6½". Calouste Gulbenkian Museum, Lisbon

Lalique's work plays on the tension between
one's distaste for the subject and one's attraction
to the beauty of his design. Here, for example,
two large somber-hued insects, quite realistically
rendered, appear to be fighting over a blood-red
tourmaline, their pronged pincers extended like
some kind of medieval torture instrument.

Below:
Longhorn beetle ring. René Lalique,
French, c. 1900–1903. Gold and foiled
enamel. Austrian Museum for Applied Art,
Vienna

Spiderweb bracelet. English, 1960s.
Gold, moonstones, and diamonds, 2" high.
Primavera Gallery, New York

SCARABS

To the ancient Egyptians, the scarab, or dung beetle, was a symbol of the sun and of rebirth or eternal life. The Egyptians observed that scarab beetles, while facing east, formed balls of dung and rolled them backward through their legs in a manner that suggested the daily movement of the sun across the heavens. Because the beetles lay their eggs in or around the dung heaps, the seemingly miraculous emergence of the larvae gave rise to associations of regeneration.

For protection in this life and the life to come, Egyptians wore scarab amulets made of dried beetles, glazed faience, ivory, amber, obsidian, or various semiprecious stones. Glazed steatite, or soapstone, was very common. Most of the scarabs found in King Tut's tomb are of lapis lazuli, which is not found in Egypt but was brought from Afghanistan, more than two thousand miles away.

Kheper (literally "come into being") was the Egyptian word both for scarab and for existence, and the name of the sun god in his morning aspect was *Khepri*. The hieroglyph for existence, and for *Khepri*, is the scarab. Egyptians believed in reincarnation; therefore, the bodies of the dead had to be carefully embalmed and buried in preparation for the next life. Winged scarab amulets were also common—dung beetles could fly, and their flight suggested another connection to the world of spirits, the sky, and, by extension, the afterlife.

Roman soldiers stationed in Egypt with Caesar's legions appropriated the scarab symbol and spread it throughout the empire. They considered scarab rings good luck. The symbolism was turned on its head by the early Christians, in part because it was favored by pagans and in part because they associated beetles with filth. For them, scarabs represented death and decay.

Scarabs and other Egyptian motifs regained favor in Europe following Napoleon's campaigns in Egypt in 1798, which led to a wave of Egyptomania. The emblem of the goddess Isis was incorporated in the coat of arms of Paris. Every chic Parisian hostess furnished her salon with Empire furniture featuring gilded lion's-claw feet and female heads on the arms, in imitation of the Sphinx.

Preceding pages:
Winged scarab bangle.
Italian, c. 1865.
Gold and micromosaic,
1¼" high. Kentshire
Galleries, New York

The Sevres porcelain factory produced Egyptian-style china and table ornaments in the form of Egyptian statues and obelisks.

Throughout the nineteenth century, an interest in classical design was stimulated by continued archaeological discoveries in Egypt and Asia Minor, and by the opening of the Suez Canal in 1869. The American designer Louis Comfort Tiffany had an extensive personal collection of Egyptian objects, including a necklace made of dried scarabs, which he used as an inspiration for his own work. Many jewelers reinterpreted ancient symbols like scarabs, with or without wings, in gold, mosaic, or semiprecious stones.

Another burst of Egyptomania erupted in the 1920s, when the treasures of Tutankhamen's tomb were unearthed. Leading European jewelers revived the scarab as a favorite design element. Cartier's designers, in particular, found inspiration in the Louvre's vast Egyptian collection, which had been built in the wake of Napoleon's campaigns. Their work successfully combined historical references with an Art Deco sensibility. The low-relief style of Egyptian sculpture blended particularly well with the two-dimensional aesthetic of the period.

Authentic Egyptian scarabs are surprisingly abundant. Set in brooches, cuff links, and rings, they are thought to bring good luck to the person who wears them. Their association with ancient mysteries makes them as compelling as ever.

Ancient Egyptian scarabs of glazed steatite.
Left: Late 12th Dynasty–early 13th Dynasty (c. 1800–1750 B.C.). ⅞" long. *Right:* 19th Dynasty (c. 1295–1186 B.C.) ¹¹⁄₁₆" long. The Metropolitan Museum of Art, Purchase Edward S. Harkness Gift, 1926 (26.7.352, .713)

Opposite:
Pectoral in the shape
of Tutankhamen's first
name. Gold, lapis lazuli,
turquoise, carnelian,
green feldspar, and
calcite, 3½ x 4³⁄₁₆".
Egyptian, from
Tutankhamen's tomb.
Late 18th Dynasty
(c. 1336–1327 B.C.).
Egyptian Museum, Cairo

Right:
Bracelet. Egyptian, from
the tomb of Amenemope,
993–984 B.C. Gold,
lapis lazuli, carnelian,
greenstone, and colored
faience, 2½" high.
Egyptian Museum, Cairo

Below:

Pendant. Probably American, c. 1890. Gold,
ancient steatite scarab, cabochon sapphire,
and enamel, 3¾ x 1¾". Private Collection

Left:

Necklace.
Robert Phillips, English, 1860.
Gold, enameled beads, and agate.
James Robinson, Inc., New York

47

Belt buckle. Piel Frères, French, c. 1905–10. Brass, gilt, enamel, red stones, and glass, 1⅞ x 3¼". Hessisches Landesmuseum, Darmstadt, Germany

Beneath the enamel scarab, which is itself a propitious amulet, is a multicolored evil eye—another Egyptian symbol representing protection, good health, and salvation.

Winged scarab pectoral. Egyptian, from the tomb of Psusennes, 21st Dynasty (1039–991 B.C.). Gold, green jasper heart scarab, polychrome glass, red jasper, and feldspar, with chain of feldspar, red and green jasper, and gold. Egyptian Museum, Cairo

The central scarab represents the god Khepri, the rising sun.

Winged scarab brooch.
Cartier, French, 1925. Ancient faience
scarab set in gold and platinum,
citrines, topazes, diamonds, emeralds,
rubies, and onyx, 2¼ x 4¾".
Private Collection

Almost all of Cartier's Egyptian-influenced
designs incorporated a piece of material
that dated back to Pharaonic times,
usually, as in this case, a faience scarab,
or occasionally a portion of carved ivory
or wood.

Below:
Brooch and belt ornament. Cartier, London, 1924. Yellow gold, platinum, smoky quartz,
cabochon emeralds, ancient blue faience scarab, diamonds, and enamel, 1⅞ x 5¼".
Art of Cartier Collection, Geneva

Brooch. Cartier, London, 1924. White gold, platinum, ancient blue faience scarab, diamonds, onyx, cabochon emeralds, cabochon sapphires, cabochon ruby, and amethyst, 1⅞ x 1¾".

Art of Cartier Collection, Geneva

Necklace.
Louis Comfort Tiffany,
American, c. 1912.
Favrile glass and gold.
Louis C. Tiffany Garden
Museum, Nagoya, Japan

Necklace.
Louis Comfort Tiffany,
American, c. 1922.
Gold and lapis lazuli,
with turquoise, coral,
and lapis beads.
Private Collection,
Courtesy Macklowe Gallery
& Modernism, New York

Bracelet. Italian, c. 1865. Gold with glass scarabs, 2¼" high. James Robinson, Inc., New York

The bracelet belonged to Alice Mason, the unhappy wife of Senator Charles Sumner who fled to Rome in the wake of an extramarital affair in Washington, D.C. It was presumably bought for her by her lover, the German ambassador to the United States. The Greek inscription—THEY SAY WHATEVER THEY WANT TO SAY; LET THEM, TO ME IT DOESN'T MATTER—implies that the couple remained unrepentant despite the scandal surrounding their romance.

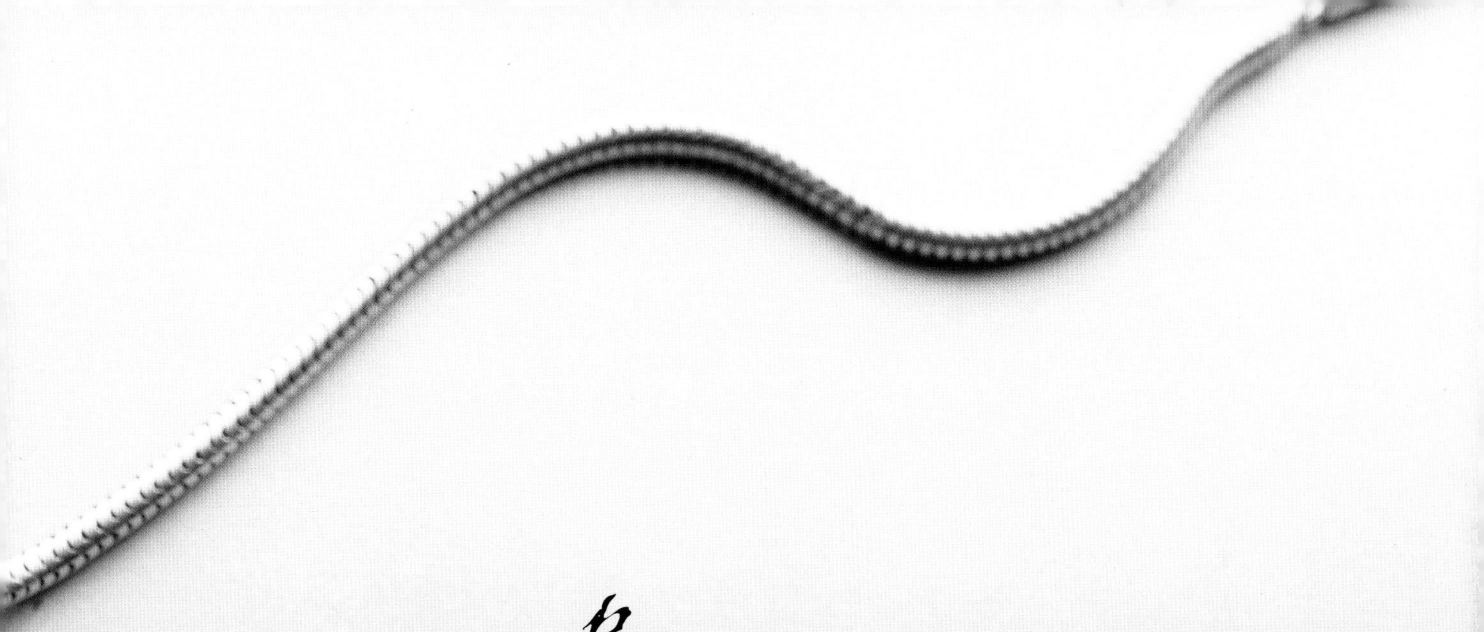

Buzzers and Stingers

Of all insects, the flying creatures that buzz, bite or sting often seem the most malevolent. A circling bee can break up a summer picnic; a persistent mosquito can banish all posibility of sleep; a taunting housefly can goad an otherwise sane person into an hourlong pursuit of the pest's demise.

Flies, mosquitoes, gnats, and midges are all members of the order Diptera. Although they appear to have only one pair of wings, a second pair has evolved into knobby organs, called *halteres,* that act as gyroscopes to maintain stability in flight.

Flies, which are thought of mainly as a nuisance, in fact probably affect human welfare, for good *and* ill, more than any other insect. Yes, they carry disease, but they also pollinate basic crops during their search for nectar. In their larval state, they clean the environment by feeding on decaying matter and aiding its decomposition. Because of this association with decay, the ancient Philistines called their god of the dead Beelzebub, Lord of the Flies; the name itself is probably onomatopoeic.

The characteristic buzz or hum of the common housefly comes from its rapid wingbeat; houseflies hum the note of F in the middle octave. The shape of a fly at rest, its wings folded to form a triangular wedge reminiscent of the stealth bomber, is always compelling to jewelers.

Bees and wasps belong to the order Hymenoptera. Wasps are frequently carnivorous; their bodies are long and slender, and the abdomen and the thorax are connected by a narrow stalk—hence the fashion term *wasp-waisted.*

The bee has long been a favorite subject of jewelers. Perhaps its most appealing aspect is its shape; perhaps it is the coloration or the association with fertilization. Two enameled black and gold bees sipping from horn flowers (page 63) evoke the beauty and serenity of the natural world. A wasp is interesting because its elongated body, marked by distinctive black and yellow bands (coloring it shares with some bees), is elegant yet menacing. Two wasps confronting each other over a piece of amber (page 70) evoke the merciless, predatory aspect of nature.

Preceding pages:
Fly necklace. c. 1880.
Crystal, emeralds, rubies,
diamonds, and gold,
on a gold chain,
each crystal ½" high.
Collection Susan B.
Kaplan

Opposite:
Bee pins. Hermès,
French, 1960s. Gold,
1" long. Susan Wingfield
Collection, Courtesy
Macklowe Gallery &
Modernism, New York

Although the small hind wings and the presence of antennae are typical of moths rather than bees, the stout furry bodies and golden color connect these insects to the bee family.

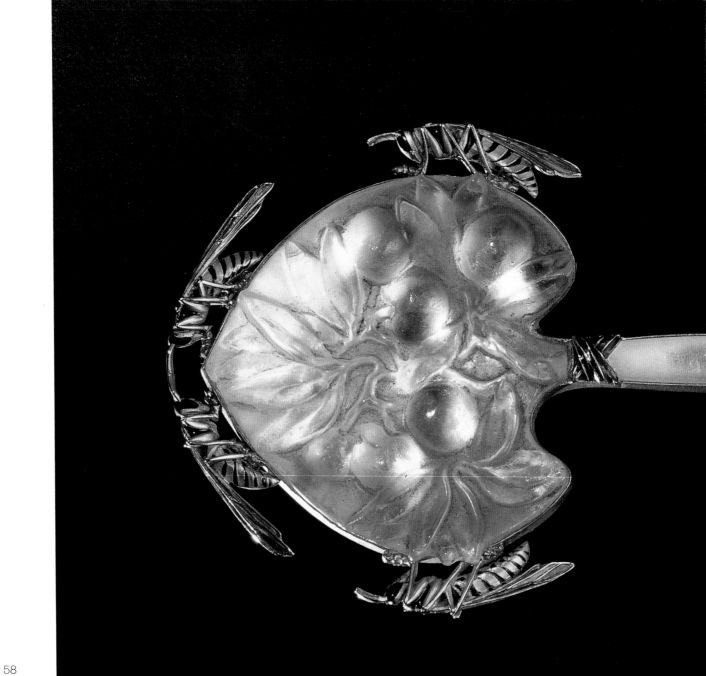

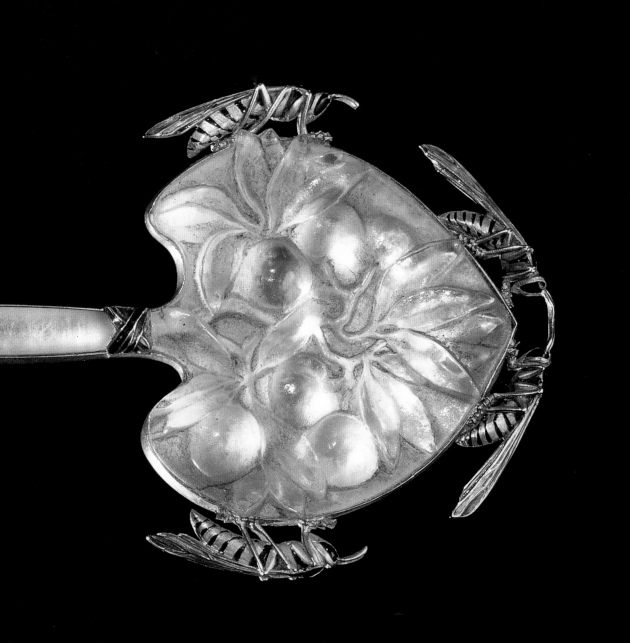

Preceding pages:
Wasp and blackthorn corsage ornament.
René Lalique, French, 1904. Gold, enamel,
and pressed glass, 1⅛ x 4½".
Musée des Arts Décoratifs, Paris

Opposite:
Bangle. English, 1875. Fifteen-karat
gold and enamel, set with diamonds,
ruby, and emerald fly on crystal,
2½" high. James Robinson, Inc.,
New York

Below:
Bee brooch. Paul Preston, British,
1979. Twenty-two- and 18-karat gold,
1½ x 1½". Private Collection

Above:
Fly locket. English, c. 1870.
Gold, with enamel, ruby, emerald, diamonds,
and crystal, with gold chain, 1½ x 1¼".
Private Collection

Left:
Bee comb. René Lalique,
French, c. 1900.
Carved and patinated horn
and enamel, 8⅛ x 6⅝".
Courtesy Sotheby's, London

Opposite:
Wasp brooch.
Paul Lienard, French,
c. 1902.
Gold, enamel, and
baroque pearls,
4½ x 3½".
Private Collection,
Philadelphia and Maine

Right:
Bee and flower comb.
Lucien Gaillard, French, 1903—4.
Horn and enamel.
Musée des Arts Décoratifs, Paris

Midge.
Ilias Lalaounis,
Greek, 1974.
Silver, obsidian, rock crystal,
malachite, and mica.
6½ x 8 x 4".
Ilias Lalaounis Jewelry
Museum, Athens, Greece

Above:

Bee and lily brooch. René Lalique, French, c. 1896–98. Abalone shell, gold, enamel, and *pâte de verre*, 1½ x 2½". Courtesy Sotheby's, London

Despite the fact that bees sting, they are generally thought of in a positive light because they pollinate flowers and many food crops and produce honey, which was humankind's only sweetener for thousands of years.

Below:

Bee brooch. Daniel Brush, American, 1981. Pure gold, 22-karat gold, 18-karat gold, steel, and diamonds, 6 x 3½". Private Collection

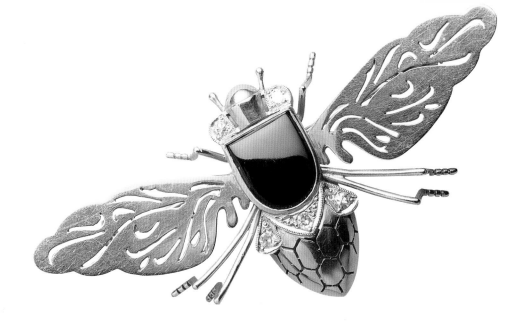

Fly brooch. French, 1930s.
Gold, onyx, and diamonds,
1½ x 2½". Private
Collection

This stylized insect most
resembles a horsefly
because of its heavy
body, big eyes, antennae,
and single pair of wings.

Right:
Fly pin.
Van Cleef & Arpels,
American, 1928.
Platinum, diamonds,
emeralds, and
sapphires, 1" long.
Primavera Gallery,
New York

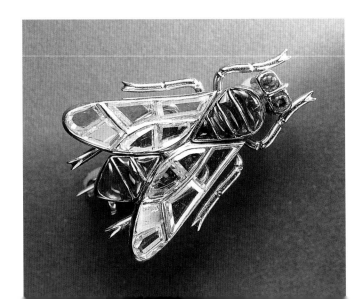

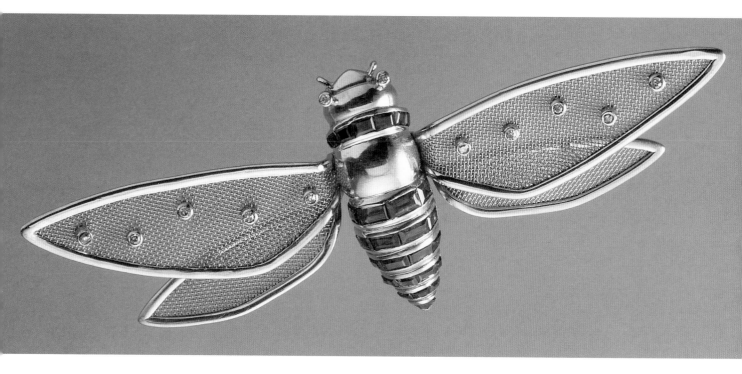

Bee clip. Boucheron,
French, 1944.
Gold, round diamonds,
and *calibré* sapphires,
1¼ x 3½".
Boucheron Collection, Paris

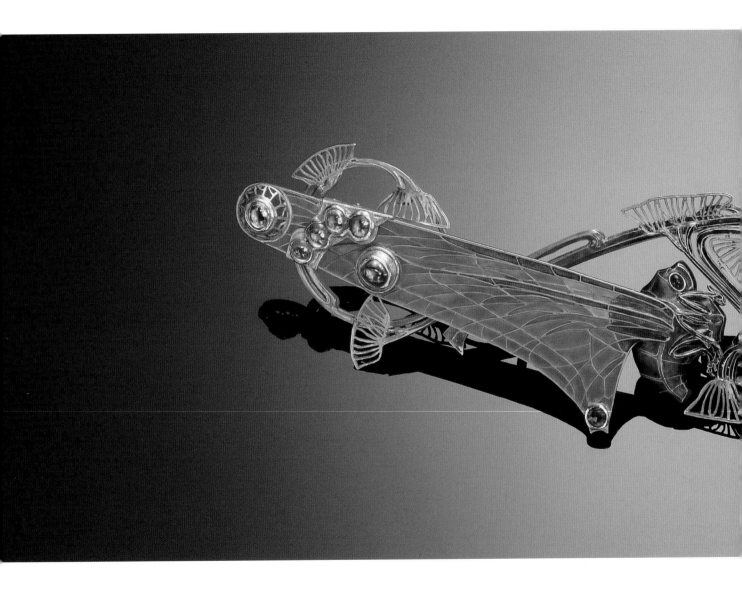

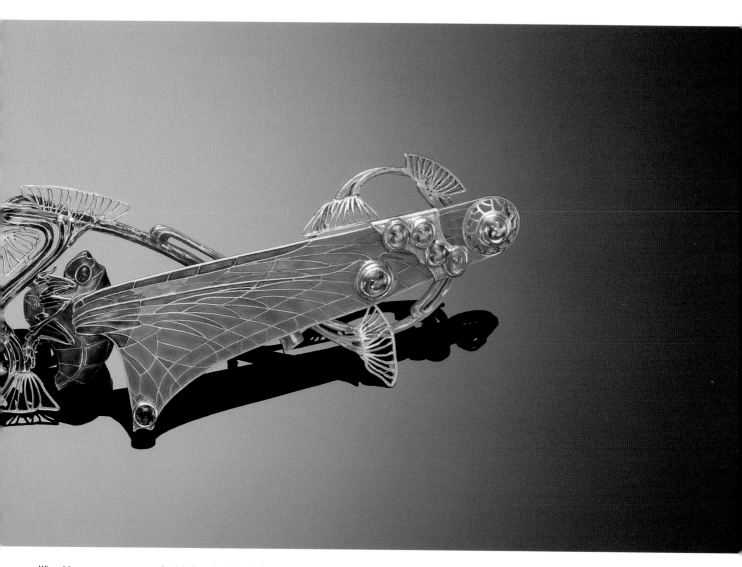

Winged-insect corsage ornament. René Lalique, French, c. 1903–5. Gold, *plique-à-jour* enamel, rubies, and peridots, 2⅛ x 8". Courtesy Sotheby's, Geneva

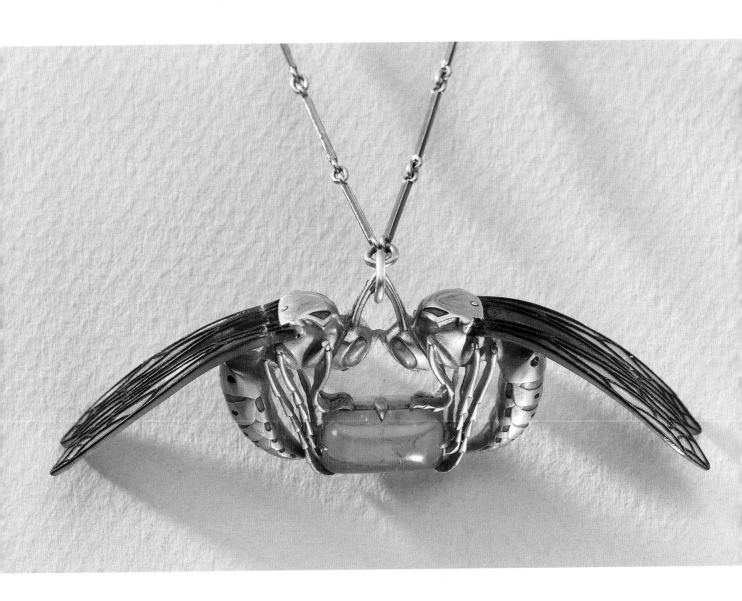

Opposite:
Wasp pendant. René Lalique,
French, c. 1900. Gold, enamel,
horn, and amber, with gold
and enamel chain, ⅞ x 3⅛".
Courtesy Sotheby's, London

Right:
Wasp pin. René Lalique,
French, c. 1899–1900. Gold,
enamel, opal, and diamonds.
The Danish Museum of
Decorative Art, Copenhagen

Left:
Hornet pendant.
From Mallia,
the royal necropolis.
Middle Minoan period
(17th century B.C.). Gold.
Archaeological Museum,
Heraklion Museum, Crete,
Greece

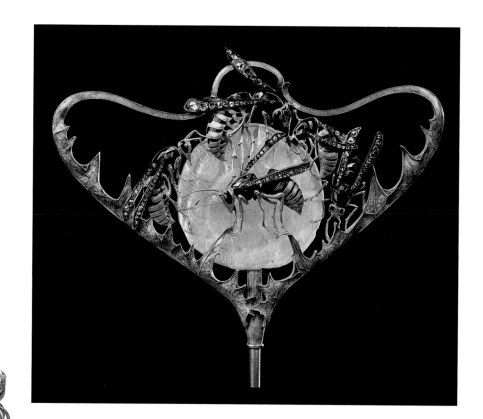

Dragonflies

Dragonflies (order Odonata) are among the oldest extant insects and were among the first animals to take flight. By the end of the Carboniferous period, about 280 million years ago, some dragonflylike insects had a wingspan of nearly two and one-half feet. During the subsequent Permian period, which was colder, modern forms of the insect began to appear. Dragonflies spend their preadult life in water; as adults, they move out of the water to feed on mosquitoes and other flying insects.

Dragonflies look delicate and dainty, but in fact they are quite voracious. Darwin called them "the tyrants of the insect world." Their astonishing eyesight plays a big part in their skill as predators. They have three simple eyes and a pair of compound eyes that can scan a field of nearly 360 degrees. They clean their eyes with a special brush attached to their front legs.

Dragonflies are gymnastic aerialists. Their four independently moving wings give them great maneuverability, and even at top speeds they can suddenly dart off in another direction. They are very fast, achieving speeds up to sixty miles per hour.

Dragonflies have long been a favorite subject for jewelers because of their distinctive silhouette and their elongated double pair of lacy, netlike wings. Victorian jewelers created formal dragonflies, with static, symmetrical wings often set with precious stones. By the turn of the century, jeweled insects had much more vitality. They seemed to hover and dart. The graceful, energetic effect was achieved through the use of materials like light brown horn or *plique-à-jour* enamel, and by setting the wings *en tremblant*.

The hair ornament of two dragonflies resting on dandelion puffballs (opposite) by Louis Comfort Tiffany is typical of Art Nouveau jewelry in that it glorifies nature in both its full beauty and its incipient sense of decay. While the dragonflies are vivid and dynamic, the dandelion flower has faded away. Tiffany achieved this remarkable effect by the use of finely worked platinum for the silken strands of the puffs. Platinum was one of Tiffany's hallmarks, and he combined it with iridium to simulate the extremely delicate gossamer wings of the dragonfly.

Preceding pages:
Brooch. Possibly English, 1880s. Sapphires, diamonds, rubies, set in gold and silvertop gold, 2½ x 3½".
Private Collection

Opposite:
Hair ornament. Louis Comfort Tiffany, American, c. 1904. Platinum, enamel, black and pink opals, and demantoid garnets, 3¼" high.
Private Collection

Right:
Brooch. Concept
by Noma Copley,
design and fabrication
by Jean Stark,
American, 1990s.
Twenty-two- and
18-karat gold,
enamel, diamonds,
tourmaline, and jade,
3 x 4". Private
Collection

Opposite:
Brooch.
Origin unknown,
c. 1915. Platinum
and diamonds,
$2\frac{1}{8}$ x $\frac{1}{2}$".
Kentshire Galleries,
New York

Above:

Brooch. French, c. 1900. Gold, enamel, and diamonds, 3 x 4".

Private Collection

Opposite:

Brooch. Louis Comfort Tiffany, American, c. 1900. Black opals, demantoid garnets, platinum, and gold, 2½ x 3". Private Collection

Brooch. Gaston Lafitte, French, 1880. *Plique-à-jour* enamel, diamonds, and rubies, set in 18-karat gold, platinum, and silver, 2¼ x 3¼". James Robinson, Inc., New York

Brooch. Italian, late 16th century. Gold, enamel, precious stones, and baroque pearl, 2½ x 3". Museo degli Argenti, Palazzo Pitti, Florence, Italy

Renaissance jewelry designers used baroque pearls with great inventiveness; in this brooch from the collection of the grand duke of Tuscany, the natural shape of the pearl simulates the elongated abdomen of the dragonfly.

Right: Brooch. Philippe Wolfers, Belgian, c. 1900. Gold, *cloisonné* and *plique-à-jour* enamels, rubies, diamonds, and pearls, 3 x 4¾". Private Collection, Philadelphia and Maine

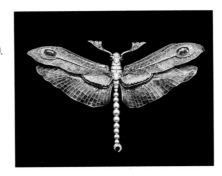

Like many jewelry designers, Wolfers took artistic license in the depiction of this insect. The wings and body are typical of dragonflies, but the large furry antennae are closer to those of moths.

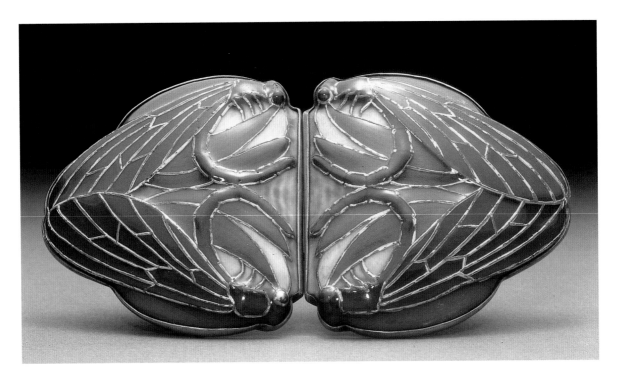

Opposite:
Waist clasp. Designed by Christian Thomsen for the Royal Copenhagen Porcelain Co.,
Danish, 1902. Silver with porcelain and gold, 2¼ x 4¼". The British Museum, London

Above:
Brooch. Roger Nachman, American, 1997.
Fused dichroic glass, 3 x 4". Private Collection

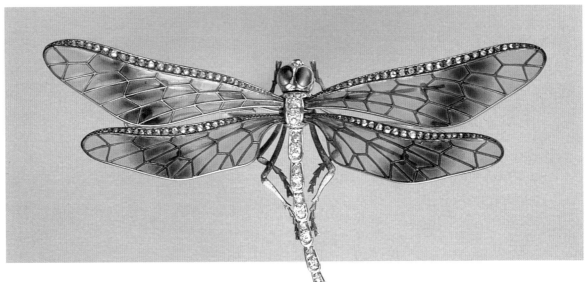

Ring.
French, c. 1900.
Gold, *plique-à-jour*
enamel, diamonds,
and rubies, 1 x ⅝".
Private Collection

Above:
Brooch.
Boucheron,
French, c. 1903.
Gold, silver, diamonds,
and enamel, 2⅜ x 3⅝".
Boucheron Collection, Paris

Right:
Pendant.
René Lalique,
French, c. 1900. Gold,
plique-à-jour enamel,
aquamarine, diamonds,
and pearls, with gold
and *plique-à-jour*
enamel chain, 2 x 3".
Macklowe Gallery &
Modernism, New York

Above:
Box. Daniel Brush, American, 1989. Pure gold, steel, spring steel, diamonds, and rare earth magnets. 1 x 1½ x 1½".
Private Collection

Belt Buckle. Piel Frères, French, c. 1900–1902. Silver, gilt, enamel, green and red stones, 2½ x 2½".
Museum für Natur und Stadtkultur, Schwäbisch-Gmünd, Germany

Brooch. European, c. 1850. Enamel, natural pearls, and diamonds, 4 x 5". Private Collection

Winged Women

The juxtaposition of women and insects in a single piece of jewelry was one of the great innovations of Art Nouveau designers. For centuries the female body had been excluded from the design vocabulary of jewelry. It was considered bad taste for one woman to wear the naked image of another woman. But Art Nouveau designers turned the subject of Woman—her face or her unclothed body—into one of their most startling and popular motifs.

Not coincidentally, this revolution in art took place just as the social position of women and women's sense of themselves were being transformed. Although flappers and suffragettes were not to appear for several decades, women were becoming increasingly active in their demands for greater equality and freedom. As the nineteenth century drew to a close, flamboyant women like Sarah Bernhardt and La Belle Otero encouraged Art Nouveau jewelers to create increasingly outrageous designs, the more erotic or bizarre the better.

René Lalique is said to have been the first goldsmith since the late Renaissance to represent the female nude in jewelry. Other daring fin-de-siècle themes included snakes, exotic winged creatures like bats, peacocks, and insects, and, most shocking of all—the winged female nude.

Lalique's winged females, like many of his images, go beyond the expression of full maturity in organic life to the next stage, which is decay. Such pieces capitalize on the unsettling combination of sexuality and death. Nowhere is this more evident than in the famous dragonfly corsage ornament (page 95) he completed in 1898. A woman—naked to the waist—protrudes from the top of a dragonfly's body; is she being swallowed whole or spit out? Her arms have metamorphosed into insect wings. The dragonfly has two outsized gold claws extended as if ready to pounce or tear a victim to shreds. This piece, perhaps more than any other, combines all the themes and potentialities of the Art Nouveau obsession with the female—she is one with nature and yet does not exist in a natural form; she is sublime and predatory; she is eternal while at the same time in transition from one mythic state to another.

Preceding pages:
Brooch. René Lalique,
French, c. 1900.
Gold and *plique-à-jour*
enamel, ½ x 3".
Private Collection

Right:
Brooch.
Eugène Feuillâtre,
French, c. 1902.
Gold, moonstones,
diamonds, pearl, and
enamel, 2¾ x 2¾".
Hessisches
Landesmuseum,
Darmstadt, Germany

The translucent
downturned wings of
an emperor moth cloak
the head of a young
woman.

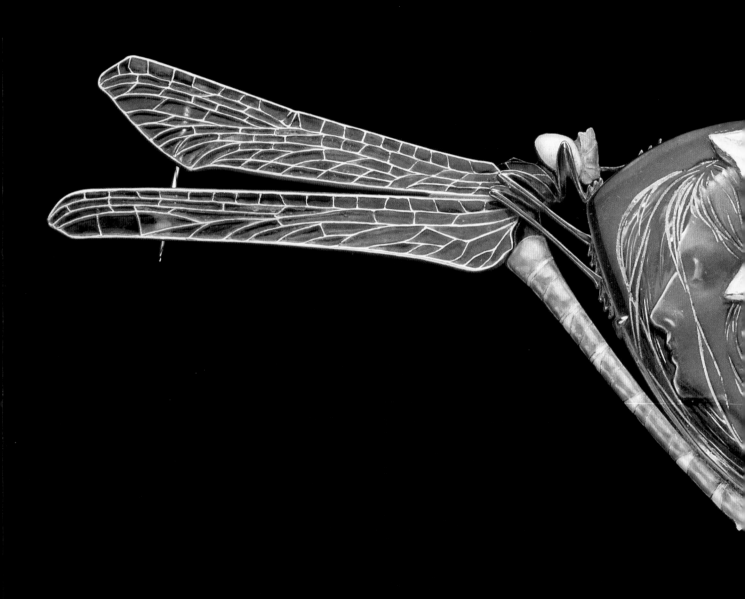

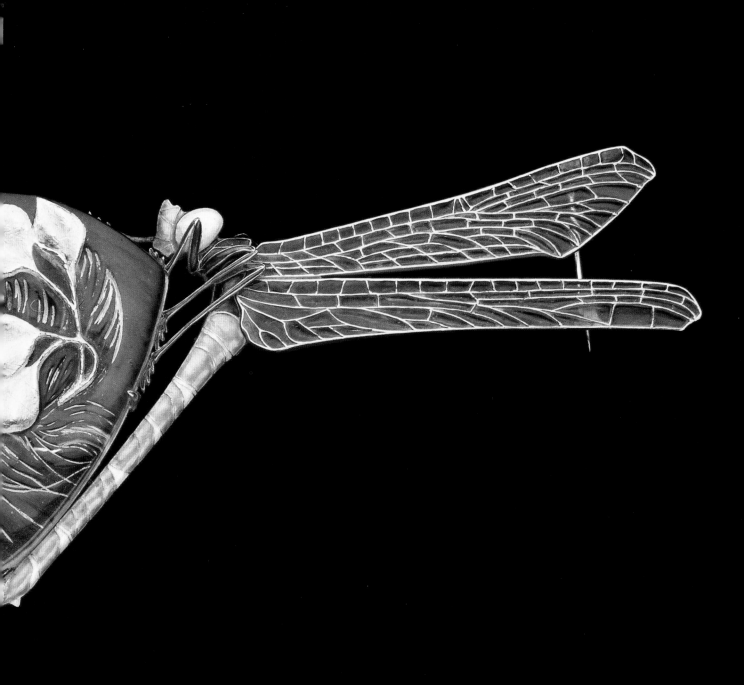

Above:
Brooch.
C. Duguine,
French, c. 1904.
Gold, *plique-à-jour*
enamel, rubies,
emeralds, and
diamonds.
Hessisches
Landesmuseum,
Darmstadt, Germany

Right:
Brooch.
Otto Prutscher,
Viennese, c. 1901.
Gold-plated silver, opals,
and enamel, 1½ x 1⅞".
Schmuckmuseum, Pforzheim,
Germany

Preceding pages:
Brooch/cloak clasp.
René Lalique, French, c. 1904–5.
Gold, glass intaglio, and *plique-à-jour*
enamel, 2 x 6⅝". Sotheby's, London

Two dragonflies hover around the head
of a water nymph, whose long hair is
entwined with leaves. The muted colors
suggest a woodland lake in autumn.

Opposite:
Corsage ornament.
René Lalique, French, c. 1897–98.
Gold, enamel, chrysoprase, moonstones,
and diamonds, 9½ x 10⅞".
Calouste Gulbenkian Museum, Lisbon

Pendant.
Probably French,
c. 1900. Gold,
plique-à-jour enamel,
and diamonds, with
gold chain, 1¾ x 2⅜".
Private Collection

Below:
Brooch.
Gaston Lafitte,
French, 1904.
Gold, *plique-à-jour*
enamel, and diamonds,
3¼ x 4". Private Collection.
Courtesy Macklowe Gallery
& Modernism, New York

Brooch.
Whiteside & Blank, American,
c. 1900. Gold, diamonds, enamel,
and *plique-à-jour* enamel, 1⅞ x 1⅝".
The Newark Museum, Newark, New Jersey

Pendant.
French, c. 1900.
Gold, diamonds,
and sapphires,
3¼ x 3".
Private Collection,
Philadelphia and
Maine

Opposite:
Brooch.
Fleuret, French,
c. 1900.
Gold, enamel,
and *plique-à-jour*
enamel, 2½ x 2½".
Macklowe Gallery
& Modernism,
New York

Right:
Pendant.
Max Friedrich Koch,
German, c. 1900. Gold,
diamonds, enamel, and
pearls, 3¼ x 2½".
Schmuckmuseum,
Pforzheim,
Germany

Butterflies and Moths

utterflies represent nature at its most playful; they come in every shade of the spectrum and every imaginable combination of hues. The coloring of butterflies evolved at least in part to spark sexual interest. It also plays a role in the protection of certain species: some butterflies, in their caterpillar stage, have eaten plants that make them toxic to their predators. Their coloring is what scientists call *aposematic*—it is a reminder to birds that may have feasted on another of their species: "Eating me will make you sick!"

Butterflies and moths make up a large order of insects known as Lepidoptera—Greek for "scaled wings"—because tiny scales cover their wings and bodies. Surprisingly, of the 250,000 species of Lepidoptera, nearly 90 percent are moths. Butterflies, which probably evolved from moths more than 50 million years ago, attract more attention because they are vividly colored day fliers, whereas most moths are more drably colored and are active at night.

Nothing in the earlier stages of a butterfly's life cycle presages what it will look like as an adult. The butterfly egg hatches into a larval, wormlike stage called a *caterpillar*. Caterpillars eat leaves and experience rapid growth, molt several times, and then stop feeding. Each caterpillar forms a sac called a *pupa*, or *chrysalis*, from which it emerges in a completely new form as an adult butterfly. This astounding metamorphosis led many ancient civilizations to represent butterflies as a symbol of life, death, and rebirth.

At least since the Renaissance, butterflies have been the most popular subject for insect jewelry, because of their physical beauty and their spiritual and ethereal associations. Many pieces from the eighteenth and early nineteenth centuries are quite beautiful, but, pinned on a woman's shoulder, they seem as earthbound as specimens mounted in a display case. Subsequently, jewelers devised ways to set stones on the ends of stiff yet flexible wires that quivered to simulate the butterfly's characteristic delicate, fluttering motion. Such *en tremblant* settings were made of light and flexible steel, and the best of these jeweled butterflies seem poised for flight.

Preceding pages:
Butterfly pins. American, except third from right, which is Russian, 1870s and 1880s. Fourteen-karat gold, enamel, and stones, 1" to 2" wide. Private Collection

Opposite:
Moth brooch and butterfly earring set. English, 1870–80. Gold, scallop shell, and pearls. *Brooch:* 1¼ x 1¾"; *earrings:* ¾". Kentshire Galleries, New York

The chubby body of the brooch suggests a moth, whereas the position of the wings on the earrings suggests butterflies.

Butterfly brooches.

Top: Gattle & Co., American. Diamond, rubies, and demantoid garnets, 1⅛ x 2⅝".

Middle: English. Diamonds, demantoid garnets, and rubies, 1⅜ x 2⅛".

Bottom: English. Diamonds, rubies, emeralds, and natural pearls, 1⅞ x 2½".

All c. 1880.

A La Vieille Russie, New York

Butterfly pendant/brooch. Henri and Paul Vever, French, c. 1900. Gold, enamels, diamonds, and pearl, 2⅜ x 4¼". Sotheby's, London

Butterfly clip. Boucheron, French, 1907. Diamonds, platinum, and gold, 1¼ x 3¼". Boucheron Collection, Paris

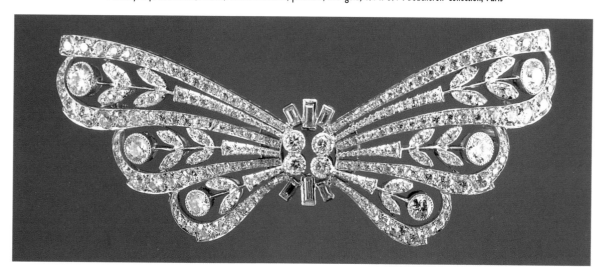

Butterfly brooch. Eugène Feuillâtre, French, c. 1900. Gold and silver, *plique-à-jour* enamel, cabochon sapphires, diamonds, and cabochon rubies, 2 x 3". James Robinson, Inc., New York

Swallowtail butterfly brooch. English, c. 1890. Silvertop gold, *guilloche* enamel, diamonds, and rubies, 2 x 3¼". Private Collection

Left:
Butterfly brooch.
René Boivin, French, 1985. Yellow gold,
white diamonds, cognac-tinted diamonds,
sapphires, and emeralds, 2 x 2⅜". Asprey, Paris

Below:
Butterfly brooch. American, c. 1920. Butterfly wings, crystal,
platinum, and diamonds, 3½" wide. Private Collection

The real butterfly pressed between pieces of crystal is
a red-spotted purple, *Limenitus astyanas* (Fabricius),
a common North American species.

Below:
Butterfly brooch.
Ralph Esmerian,
American, 1998.
Diamonds,
yellow diamonds,
and steel, 3 x 4".
R. Esmerian,
New York

107

Left:
Butterfly earrings.
English, c. 1860.
Gold and *pietra dura*
(semiprecious stones), 2¼" long.
James Robinson, Inc., New York

Below:
Butterfly brooch.
Mauboussin, French, 1965.
Gold, cloissoné enamel,
engraved emeralds,
cabochon rubies, brilliants,
and sapphires,
4 x 3¼".
Mauboussin, Paris

Left:
Butterfly brooch
with watch.
Alexis Falize,
enamel by A. Tard,
French, 1875.
Gold and enamel,
4¼ x 1¼".
James Robinson, Inc.,
New York

Butterfly pins. Origin
unknown, c. 1890.
Enamel, diamonds,
and pearls. ½ x 1¾".
Private Collection

Butterfly belt buckle. Child & Child,
English, c. 1900. Enamel on silver, 1½ x 3".
Private Collection

Above:
African moth pendant.
John Paul Miller,
American, 1994.
Gold with enamel
on pure gold, 2½" wide.
Private Collection

Right:
Moth brooch.
Mario Buccellati,
Italian, c. 1940–50.
Multicolored gold,
1½ x 1¾".
Kentshire Galleries,
New York

Above:

Butterfly and octopus brooch.
Designed by Wilhelm Lucas von Cranach
for Louis Werner, German, 1900.
Gold, pearls, diamonds, rubies,
amethysts, topaz, and enamel,
3¾ x 3¼". Schmuckmuseum,
Pforzheim, Germany

Right:
Butterfly comb.
Designed by Charles Desrosiers
for Georges Fouquet,
French, 1898–99.
Tortoiseshell, gold,
amethyst, opals,
and diamonds,
6¼ x 3½".
Musée du Petit
Palais, Paris

Butterfly brooch. Louis Aucoc,
French, c. 1900. Gold, diamonds,
enamel, and horn. Museum für
Kunsthandwerk, Frankfurt, Germany

Swallowtail butterfly buckle. René Lalique, French, c. 1903–4.
Gold, enamel, sapphire, and opal, 2⅞ x 7¼".
The Anderson Collection, University of East Anglia,
Norwich, England

Right:
Pendant with two butterflies
and a flower. Austrian, c. 1900.
Gold, enamel, and diamonds,
4 x 2½".
Private Collection

Butterfly brooch. JAR,
American, 1987. Platinum,
sapphires, and diamonds,
3 x 4¼". Private Collection

Above:

Butterfly pins. English, c. 1865. Scottish agate and silver, all 2 x 3". Collection Ginny R. Dawes, New York

Below:

Butterfly brooch. Peter Carl Fabergé, Russian, c. 1908. Gold, enamel, diamonds, sapphires, and rubies. Private Collection, Philadelphia and Maine

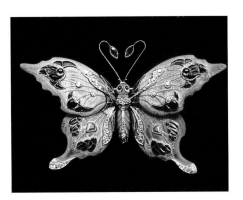

Left:

Butterfly brooch. Designed by René Lalique for Louis Aucoc, French, c. 1900. Horn, enamel, rubies, and diamonds, 2¾ x 3½". Private Collection, Philadelphia and Maine

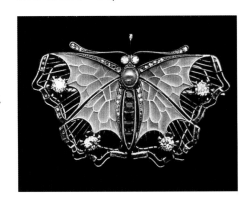

Below and page 116:
Butterfly brooch and clips. Cartier, French, 1945.
Yellow gold, enamel, coral, emeralds, and diamonds.
Brooch: 1¾ x 3¼"; clips: ¾ x 1½".
Courtesy Art of Cartier Collection, Geneva

ACKNOWLEDGMENTS

In 1990, when we began working on *Cuff Links,* our first joint project and first book about jewelry, we were fortunate enough to elicit the guidance of a particularly generous group of experts in the field. A decade later, our gratitude for and dependence on the continuing counsel of Ralph Esmerian, Penny Proddow and Marion Fasel, Brian Albert and Joe Ahumado, Joyce Jonas, and Janet Zapata is undiminished.

Many jewelers, jewelry designers, and collectors were gracious enough to share their knowledge with us and to either permit us to photograph pieces in their collections or provide photographs of them. Among those, we would like to thank the following: Joan Boening, Edward and Norma Munves, and Damon Powell of James Robinson, Inc.; Peter Schaffer, Rose Casella, and Adam Patrick of A La Vieille Russie; Haim Manischevitz, Audrey Friedman, and Michael Berna of Primavera; Barbara Macklowe and Ben Macklowe of Macklowe Gallery & Modernism; Janet Mavec of J. Mavec & Company; Marcie Immerman, Ellen Israel, and Jeanie Birmingham of Kentshire Galleries; Ward Landrigan of Verdura; Elli Antoniades of Ilias Lalounis; Camilla Dietz Bergeron; Daniel and Olivia Brush; Noma Copley; Ginny and Tom Dawes; John Paul Miller; Dr. & Mrs. Joseph Sataloff; and David Weinstein.

We are also grateful for the help of Dr. Fritz Falk of the Schmuckmuseum in Pforzheim, Germany; Ulrike von Hase-Schmundt of Munich; Anne-Christine Amgwerd at the Art of Cartier Collection, Geneva; Philippe Garner of Sotheby's, London; Kieran McCarthy of Wartski, London; Duncan Semmens from Hancocks, London; Kay Poludniowski of the Sainsbury Centre for Visual Arts, University of East Anglia, Norwich, England; Barbara Cartlidge, London; Diana Scarisbrick, London; Antonio Quattrone, Florence; Pascale Karam at Asprey, Paris; Michel Tonnelot of Boucheron, Paris; and Marguerite de Cerval of the Mauboussin Archive, Paris.

Simon Taylor of Art Resource, New York; Deanna Cross at the Photograph Library of The Metropolitan Museum of Art; Stephane Houy-Townes from the Costume Institute Library of The Metropolitan Museum of Art; and Martin Durrant of the V&A Picture Library guided our search through the resources of their collections and expedited our every request. Carole Kismaric, as always, helped us visualize our concepts for this book.

Jeweled Bugs and Butterflies draws on the fascination and allure of insects, and we wish to thank Dr. Kefyn Catley of the American Museum of Natural History in New York for providing us with a wealth of information about Insecta and Arachnida and for correcting our numerous misconceptions about his favorite subject.

We are delighted to acknowledge our wonderful continuing relationship with our editor Harriet Whelchel, our designer Carol Robson, and president and publisher Paul Gottlieb at Abrams. And finally, we offer special thanks to John Parnell who did the principal photography for *Jeweled Bugs and Butterflies.* John's wit, intelligence, and sensitivity illuminated and expanded our own vision of this compelling subject.

INDEX

Page numbers in italics refer to illustrations

PHOTOGRAPH CREDITS

All photographs are by John Parnell
with the following exceptions:

Anonymous credit: 52, 63 left, 82 top, 99 top,
    114 bottom left, 114 bottom right.
Art of Cartier Collection: endpapers, 29 bottom,
    50 bottom, 51, 115, 116.
Austrian Museum for Applied Art: 37 bottom.
Asprey, Paris: endpapers, 107 top.
Behl, David: 50 top, 107 bottom, 112 right.
Brandon-Jones, Michael: 112 bottom left.
Brooklyn Museum of Art: 9.
Boucheron Collection: 67, 84 top, 105 bottom.
The British Museum: 82 bottom.
Calouste Gulbenkian Museum: 24–25 center,
    37 top, 95.
Dawes, Tom: 114 top.
Electrum, London: 61 bottom.
Fernandez, Manuel: 108 bottom right.
Forman, Werner/Art Resource: 6, 45, 49.
Fotograf Ole Woldbye: 71 top.
Fotostudio Gunther Meyer, Pforzheim: 36 right,
    94 bottom, 111 left.
Giraudon/Art Resource: 44.
Goodbody, Richard: 53 top.

Hessisches Landesmuseum, Darmstadt: 48, 91, 94 top.
Macklowe Gallery & Modernism: endpapers, 97 left,
    98.
The Metropolitan Museum of Art: 34, 43, 75; Bob
    Hanson, 31 bottom.
Miller, John Paul: 22–23, 110 left.
Museum für Kunsthandwerk, Frankfurt: 112 top left.
Museum für Natur und Stadtkultur,
    Schwäbisch-Gmünd: 86 bottom.
The Newark Museum/Art Resource: 97 right.
Pierrain/Photothèque des Musées de la Ville
    de Paris: 111 right.
Quattrone, Antonio, Florence: 81.
Ilias Lalounis, New York: 64.
Scarisbrick, Diana, London: 25 top.
Schmuckmuseum, Pforzheim: 99 right.
Sotheby's, Geneva: 68–69.
Sotheby's, London: binding front, 36 left, 62, 65 top,
    70, 92–93, 105 top.
Sully-Jaulmes, L. / Musée des Arts Décoratifs: 58–59,
    63 right.
TAP Service, Ministry of Culture, Hellenic Republic,
    Athens: 71 bottom.
Taylor, John Bigelow: 65 bottom, 77, 86 top.
Verdura: 31 top.